MOVE

From Despondency to Destiny
Your Destiny awaits!

Frizella Taylor

TaylorMade Publishing

www.TaylorMadePublishingFL.com

Unless otherwise indicated, all scripture references are from
King James Version (KJV)
The Amplified Bible (AMP)
New Living Translation (NLT)
New International Version (NIV)
The Message (MSG)
The Passion Translation (TPT)

MOVE From Despondency to Destiny Your Destiny Awaits
ISBN: 978-0-9968123-4-4, copyright © 2019

Cover Photo Paul Smith on Unsplash

FRIZELLA TAYLOR
Jacksonville, FL, USA

All rights reserved under International copyright law. Contents and or cover may not be reproduced in whole or part in any form without the express written consent of the publisher.

For additional copies, please visit our website:
www.frizelladonegantaylor.com
www.taylormadepublishingfl.com

Table of Contents

Preface i

Introduction iv

Chapter 1: What is the Issue? 1

Chapter 2: How to Understanding Divine Appointment 11

Chapter 3: How Does God Guide Me? 19

Chapter 4: How do I Follow the Voice of God? 29

Chapter 5: Arriving in Destiny! 38

Chapter 6: How to Stay on Destiny Track 47

Chapter 7: Healing in the Emotions 60

Word from the Lord! 69

Poem: He Can Be Found 72

About the Author 74

About the Publisher 76

Books by Frizella 77

Preface

Over the years I have experienced many trials and tribulations, some of them felt as though they would take me out. Somehow, in my heart, I knew God had a plan for me. The problem was, I did not know the full plan and I did not understand the direction He was taking me.

Perhaps, if I had known, I may not have wanted to continue, or I would have tried to intercept God's plan and go in a different direction. Either way, I moved across the other side of pain, disappointment, divorce, loss of my mom and many other roads and into most of my destiny. When I think of destiny, I see myself moving forward on an open road. As I travel the road, I can see the issues from my past as signs and flashing lights on the road. I just kept moving past them leaving each one behind me.

Does that mean I will never experience pain or disappointments again? Of course not. At least now, I know how to deal with them and how Father God will bring me through and continue to move me through to Destiny! You too have a divine appointment. Destiny awaits you, are you coming?

The Lord helps us in many ways, this scripture from Psalms 32:8 says, "I will instruct you and teach you in the way you should go; I will counsel you with my loving eye on you." First, He will instruct or direct us, by providing us with direction. Then, He will teach us, by imparting knowledge and skills. He will counsel us with the interchange of opinions as to future guidance.

We can see that the Lord cares enough about us that He makes sure we can handle the knowledge and information that He provides. He keeps His eyes on us to ensure we stay on track. One thing I have learned about the Lord is that He is a gentleman. He does not force us to follow Him but allows us to choose to follow His leading. So when I got off the path, it was my choice, my decision, to try to follow what others were doing or what my selfish desires were leading me to.

However, God loved me too much to leave me there. He provided me a way to get back into His presence and grace. It was first through repentance and a turning away from the things that caused me to move away from Him. After I did that, I made a decision that I wanted to do the will of the Lord. Ever since I made that decision, He has proved himself as my provider, my confidant and my all in all. He is the one I lean on when times are hard. He keeps me from falling back into the dark places of my life from where He delivered me. So, get ready to be challenged to move from despondency to destiny as the Lord ministers to you. Allow the words in this book to invite you to a new or continual experience in HIM.

Introduction

As you move through life, you find that situations, issues failures, and success are inevitable. "Things in life happens." Some things are good and some things are bad. Regardless of which situation you are in today, do not allow it to stop you from pursuing God and the things that He has for you to do.

These situations and circumstances will get in the way of your progress and prevent you from moving forward. When this happens, you have to figure out how to move pass your past so you can move into your destiny. Your destiny is connected to a divine appointment as ordered by the Lord. Therefore, maneuvering through life becomes a timely manner. It all depends on the Lord's timing and your willingness to follow the path be puts before you.

In this book, we will look at, discuss, and discover what "Move, From Despondency to Destiny, Your Destiny Awaits" means. What is it? How do you recognize it? How do you respond to it? Moreover, why should you respond to it? "It", is your past, your destiny. Then, we will look at ways in which God can guide you into your destiny using divine appointments. Further, we will learn how to know that God is leading and how to not miss HIM.

Lastly, we will learn and understand how to hear God's voice, and follow His leading. With this in mind, you will be able to walk into your destiny and not allow life's pressure to deter you.

Chapter 1: What is the Issue?

When you are trying to move forward in life, sometimes you hit some obstacles along the way. Obstacles appear in many forms, shapes, situations or circumstances. In order to protect yourself, you subsequently block out painful things or incidents that have happened in the past.

I do not know about you but I can definitely identify with blocking out pain in an effort to avoid feeling it anymore. However, the issue with that is the pain is still there and it manifests itself in different ways or other areas of your life. For instance, when you are hurt from a past relationship due to the other person's infidelity you block out the pain or even the fact that it ever happened. Then, in subsequent relationships, you find that you are unable to trust the new person. This shows that you are allowing past pain to prevent you from moving forward. So, let us discuss some common issues that stand in the way of destiny…

> Try to identify the pain area that is holding you back.

- ➢ Non-marital relationships
- ➢ Marriage / Divorce
- ➢ Death of loved one(s)
- ➢ Emotional issues
- ➢ Persecution by others

Non-marital Relationships

These are relationships with your friends, co-workers, relatives, neighbors, church folks or even a total stranger. Regardless, everyone wants to experience good relationships and people encounters. It does not matter if it is with a close friend or total stranger.

In these relationships, you "hang out" or "kick it" together. Chatting, having fun, eating great meals and even vacationing together. The point is you have these awesome relationships, then something happens, a derogatory statement is made, a comment is misinterpreted, a strange look is given or received, etc…

Let us use a coworker as an example; a misunderstanding happens that causes friction between you and the other person. The friction escalates into a big fallout between the two of you. You have to work with this person every day and the issue causes work distractions. Then your work begins to suffer and the rumors start. Now your manager is involved.

What seemed like a little issue has escalated into a bigger issue. The issue affects your work, it affects your raise and your promotion…you are stunted. You are unable to move forward in your destiny as it pertains to your career.

Marriage / Divorce

There are good marriages and there are not so good marriages. We will look at both as examples of how each of them can adversely affect you moving forward in your destiny.

If you find yourself in a marriage that is seemingly breaking down, you tend to breakdown with it. The pain from marital problems and issues sometimes become unbearable and can stop you in your tracks. You go from happy to miserable in a very short amount of time.

For example, when you are working in ministry and marital issues crop up, it can affect you to the point where you are not able to pray. This means the issue has bled through into your ministry. Your prayer life suffers because your marital problems have consumed all of your energy.

The tone of your message and your approach to people starts to change. The way you preach and teach changes and becomes harsh, hard or judgmental. You are no longer ministering to the people, but you are ministering out of your hurts and pains. Hurting people hurt people!

At home, your children begin to feel the tension from the issues. The insurmountable pain you are experiencing is taken out on them, even when it is not your intentions. Marital problems tend to affect many areas of your life. It can even introduce an element of fear when abuse is involved. Fear of what your spouse will, or can do to cause potential harm or danger. You can experience an inability to sleep and a loss of appetite. You can also experience various levels of anxiety and depression.

However, everyone's situation is different and each person deals with marital problems in different ways. How the problem affects you may not be the same as how it affects another person. Why, because some people's level of tolerance is higher or lower than another's tolerance in a similar situation. The bottom line is marital problems disrupt your destiny and prevent you from moving forward, it is a roadblock to progression.

Similarly, many divorce problems can mimic many of the same marital problems. The emotions associated with divorce and marital problem are failure, brokenness, loneliness, despair, and rejection, to name a few. Regardless of how bad the relationship is/or was the pain from a divorce still exists. You cannot help but replay in your mind the process of starting over, moving, or giving up friends once shared. Sometimes you even have to change churches or your place of employment just to find solace.

> *Emotions from divorce: failure, brokenness, loneliness, despair*

Divorce sometimes changes your financial and social status. You may not be able to afford to live the way you did on two salaries. Your friends / social groups change when you no longer share the same friends or run in the same circles. Therefore, friends have to choose you or your ex-spouse. These things change or shift your destiny.

Divorce can change a lot about you. It shifts your destination and forces you to take a different path. However, that does not change who you are, or what God has called you to do. You simply must go in a different direction or route to get to your destination. Therefore, the change may lengthen or shorten your destination but it should not stop you. Regardless, you still must fulfill your individual calling.

Unfortunately, due to the divorce you may endure a healing process that may take you "off the grid" for a season. While this may not be the worst relationship you have experienced, it is still painful and you really do feel the effects of it.

On the other side, how does a good marriage disrupt your destiny? That is a good question. You would think it would not, but it most certainly will in a subtle way. I will use myself as an example.

Before I met my current husband, I knew God had called me to write and publish Christian books. I had already ordered 10 ISBN numbers and published two books. I was working on the third book when he came along. Meeting him was indeed a whirlwind, mainly because I had settled on not marrying again. I was happy doing my own thing and serving the Lord.

As fate would have it, the year we met on my birthday in February. I reluctantly gave him my number and he called the next day and every day after. In April, we were engaged and the same year, we got married in July! I experienced an exuberance of happiness, in fact, so happy that I put my book to the side. You can say I got distracted at becoming a wife.

I was supposed to write and publish the third book in 2017. I struggled to focus on my book, writing a little here and there. By the end of the year, my husband and I decided I had better get this done. We began to work together. I wrote and typed while he and my sister edited and proofed. We got it done, written and published mid-spring of 2018!

You see, being happily married really can disrupt your destiny even when you and your spouse have a joint destiny together as a couple. Understand there are times when one or the other will have a pre-planned destiny that was in flight before being connected. Therefore, there should be some thought in continuing to fulfill your destiny so that it is not aborted. The last thing you want is to stand before the Lord and say I did not obey you because I was being a spouse. You can do both.

Death of a loved one

We all know too well that when we lose a loved one it is devastating and it seems like the world stops moving. Especially when you were very close to them. Their death sometimes brings pain and sorrow that becomes so overwhelming until you find yourself unable to move forward. The tears flow out of nowhere!

The one thing that you are not thinking about is your destiny. Why? Because for some, you cannot or do not see your future without your loved one. You wonder how life can go on. How can I do this without him or her? You do not want to get out of bed, let alone go to work.

The grief you are feeling concerning your loved one seems to be too much to bear. You may feel isolated, angry, lost or even lonely. You should be careful not allow anxiety and depression to overtake you.

Death of a loved one is like a divorce in that it too can alter your social status and the course of your life. If your loved one was the sole provider and your source of income and they took care of all the family matters, then the effects of losing them is total blow to your lifestyle.

Here, again, you must start over or learn to continue without your loved one. You do not have them to do the task for you, nor do you have them to consider in planning your next move or steps. You have to deal with what you feel or think they would do in certain situations. Therefore, the loss of loved ones can potentially stop the progression of your destiny.

Persecution by Others

When others persecute you, it can take various forms but in the end, the effects are the same. Certainly, you can relate to persecution against you by someone. Persecution is the act of being harassed or oppressive treatment inflicted on you; it is the act of being taunted or targeted by someone. This is behavior toward a person in an effort to discredit them and make others believe this individual is a bad person or a person who they feel you should not associate with.

In today's term, simply put, believers persecute others right in the church. Some folks receive persecution from non-believers, believing family members, as well as from former friends. Lies are told about who they are, or what they said is misinterpreted. Either way persecution happens.

Overall, to experience persecution is an ultimate way of killing a person's character. Persecution is designed to stop you from fulfilling what God called you to do. It makes you feel incompetent, worthless and useless. When you are under the effects of this state of mind or state of being, you begin to question yourself. "Did God really call me? Am I supposed to be doing this or am I even capable of doing this?"

Now, self-doubt has infringed on you and your destiny is in jeopardy. Why, because as a target you begin to believe the lie about who you are and doubt who God called you to be or to do. The inner battle of self-esteem is going on within the battlefield of the mind, the battle of the heart and the battle of self-worth. All of which will definitely hinder your destiny.

We covered quite a bit of information in order to discover some ways in which your destiny could to be interrupted, stopped, or even delayed. How do you get back on track, start again or get around the issues? Sometimes, it is nothing more than God intervening on your behalf to pull you out!

Chapter 2: How to Understand Divine Appointment

A divine appointment is an incident or happen stance of meeting or encountering something that seems so bizarre that only God can arrange it. It is an apparent coincidental encounter or an event caused by God for some specific purpose. This purpose may not be obvious during the encounter or the purpose may become apparent sometime later. Now, let us go a little deeper to obtain a fuller understanding of what a divine appointment is from a spiritual perspective.

To understand what God has in store for you in your walk towards destiny, you must get the mind of Christ and increase your biblical knowledge of Him. In Habakkuk 2:3 it tells us, *"For the vision is yet for an appointed time..."* Here we see and understand the vision God has for you, it is for a set or an appointed time or a future time determined by God. You cannot go ahead of it nor should you get behind it, but you should stay in step with the Lord. This verse goes on to say, *"But at the end it shall speak..."* the interpretation of this portion of the scripture is a prophecy that personifies the voice of God and brings fulfillment to His plan in your life.

In addition, this verse says, *"And not lie..."* God is Truth and His word does not lie nor is it spoken in vain. His Word will not return void without accomplishing what it was meant to do. *"Wait for it"* implies you should wait in anticipation of what God has for you, without being overly anxious for its arrival. The scripture continues by saying. *"Because it will surely come. It will not tarry"* meaning, His promise will not fail to arrive.

As you can see from this scripture, you can have an expectation of God concerning His plan for your life. While waiting, you may experience some dark places in your life and you may still have struggles in some areas. Either way, you can get past those places by allowing the Word of God to guide you.

Encounters of a Divine Appointment

You do not have to feel like every moment of your life is a divine appointment, because it is not. However, you will learn to recognize those special moments, which you will come to know as a divine appointment. Mainly because it will be so bizarre, that only God would be able to arrange it.

Divine appointment(s) can happen when you are willing to allow the Holy Spirit to lead you. Most of the time, you will not know or understand why you are going in a certain direction or why you are talking to a complete stranger. However, later on you see the result of a seemingly odd direction or conversation and realize that God orchestrated it! Divine appointment lines up with divine direction. Unless you recognize the divine appointment, you cannot benefit from the divine direction.

> *Unless you recognize the divine appointment, you cannot benefit from the divine direction.*

Joshua, Moses is dead!

The Lord spoke to Joshua in the book of Joshua 1:1-3 (KJV) saying, *"After the death of Moses the servant of the Lord, it came to pass that the Lord spoke to Joshua the son of Nun, Moses' assistant, saying: ² "Moses My servant is dead. Now therefore, arise, go over this Jordan, you and all this people, to the land which I am giving to them—the children of Israel. ³Every place that the sole of your foot will tread upon I have given you, as I said to Moses."*

Surely, Joshua understood that Moses was dead; perhaps he was moping, grieving or unsure of his next move. However, God saw fit to have a divine appointment with Joshua and in this appointment not only did God remind him that His servant Moses was dead, but He also wanted to get Joshua back on track, back on assignment and back to moving forward.

In Joshua 1:2 it says, *"…Now therefore, arise, go over this Jordan, you and all this people, to the land which I am giving to them — the children of Israel,"* we see here that the Lord "spoke" to Joshua. In that moment Joshua, recognized it was the Lord speaking to him, the voice of the Lord God. Therefore, he had to obey and once he did only then he was able to benefit from the divine direction he was given.

In this case, the direction was to first "arise" or get up! God told him to go in the direction of Jordon. Therefore, when he obeyed, the Lord showed him all the land that He was giving to him. He promised him that every place the sole of his foot tread on He had already given him. This is the same promise He made to Moses just before he died in Deuteronomy chapter 34.

Saul / Paul

In Acts 9:3-6 (NKJV) the Bible says, *"As he journeyed he came near Damascus, and suddenly a light shone around him from heaven. ⁴Then he fell to the ground, and heard a voice saying to him, "Saul, Saul, why are you persecuting Me?" ⁵ And he said, "Who are You, Lord?" Then the Lord said, "I am Jesus, whom you are persecuting. It is hard for you to kick against the goads." ⁶ So he, trembling and astonished, said, "Lord, what do You want me to do?" Then the Lord said to him, "Arise and go into the city, and you will be told what you must do."*

In these verses, the Lord spoke to Saul, the person who persecuted the church by going from house to house dragging men and women of faith to prison. All the while, the disciples were still preaching Jesus. Saul was threatening the disciples of the Lord with murder and wanted letters (or permission) from the high Priest so that if he found any Christians he would bind them and bring them to Jerusalem.

However, the Lord had a plan for Saul. He met Saul on the road near Damascus. The Lord had a divine appointment setup for Saul with a bright light shining from Heaven. Imagine how Saul's heart must have skipped a few beats. The light knocked Saul to the ground, and this was such an event that even Saul a non-believer, hearing the voice of the Lord had to recognize it was the Lord. The Bible said he trembled (like afraid) and was astonished (like in disbelief) but answered with "LORD". Now, he is ready to benefit from the divine appointment and receive his divine direction.

The Lord said to Saul, Arise (get up from where you are) and Go (move forward in the direction I send you). Into the city and you will be told what you must do. You see, in this moment, Saul did not have a clue of what was waiting for him and sometimes neither do you!

Being obedient and moving forward when you do not know what is in store has more reward than you can ever think or imagine. Saul in Acts 9:8, got up from the ground and in that moment, he was blind, unable to see and others led him by hand. For three days Saul was blind; forced into a fast, he did not eat or drink anything.

Saul was in for his divine benefit! Ananias, a disciple of the Lord received a divine vision from the Lord (Acts 9:10-12). Again, the Lord said, *"Arise"* and *"Go"* (these are directives from the Lord). He sent Ananias to Straight Street to ask for

Saul of Tarsus, who was there blind and praying. Of course, like us, Ananias reminds the Lord, Saul is the man that kills Christians by the authority vested by the chief Priest. (Please understand God's authority is greater!) The Lord said to Ananias *"Go"*, because He chose Saul as His vessel. Ananias's encounter of divine appointment was to lay hands on Saul in order for him to receive his sight and be filled with the Holy Spirit. Then, he was baptized and began preaching Christ!

This account helps you to see from the scriptures how being obedient and willing to follow the leading of the Holy Spirit will allow you to experience encounters with God that will change the course of your life in the most profound ways. The Bible says in Psalms 32:8-9 (NKJV), *"[8]I will instruct you and teach you in the way you should go; I will guide you with My eye. [9]Do not be like the horse or like the mule, Which have no understanding, Which must be harnessed with bit and bridle, Else they will not come near you."* The Lord's divine direction here is that as long as you allow Him, He will instruct and teach you. He will guide and watch over you with His eye.

There must be a willingness on your part because the Lord will not force you. However, when you buck against the Lord's leading, the Word says do not be like the horse or mule, which have no understanding and must be led by a bit and bridle. This implies that you have no understanding of divine directions or divine appointment; you are all over the place.

To understand divine appointment, you must be willing to allow the Lord to endow you with spiritual wisdom. At some point after Saul's conversion to Paul, he wrote the book of Ephesians where he talks about our Lord and Savior Jesus Christ. Paul wrote a prayer on how to receive spiritual wisdom in Ephesians 1:17-22, that is still relevant today:

Heavenly father I ask you to grant me spiritual wisdom and revelation knowledge of Jesus, that my eyes of understanding will be opened and I am enlightened to know the hope of Your calling of what the riches of the glory of His inheritance are for me. I want to know and understand what is the exceeding greatness of your power toward me, who believe, according to the working of Your mighty power which works in Christ when God raised Him from the dead and seated Him at His right hand in the Heavenly places above the principality, powers, might and dominion and every name that is named, not only in this age but also in that which is to come. That everything that hinders me is put under Your feet for you gave him Jesus to be head over all things to the church In Jesus name Amen!

Chapter 3: How Does God Guide Me?

Let us establish the meaning of the word "guide". Guide is an action word or verb. It means to assist a person in travelling through or reaching a destination in an unfamiliar area. The act of guiding is by accompanying or giving direction someone. Furthermore, it is to show points of interest and explain the meaning or significance. To guide is to supply a person with advice or counsel in order to move them in a certain direction or along a designated path.

My Guiding Journey

I can recall as a young Christian trying to follow the leading of the Lord. Honestly, it did not make sense to me at all. No one I knew talked about the Lord guiding them. Somehow, before I understood what it meant to "be led" by the Lord, I always felt something or someone was talking to me, but because I did not know any better, I thought I was just talking to myself. Of course, for that reason, I never told anyone what was going on.

Then one day the Lord spoke to me about Jeremiah 1:5 and I was clueless as to what was happening with me or why I was hearing this voice. Jeremiah 1:5 KJV says, *"Before I formed thee in the belly I knew thee; and before thou camest forth out of the womb I sanctified thee, and I ordained thee a prophet unto the nations."* It was a long road before I understood what this meant. All I knew is that I loved reading the Bible as a young girl. I had a biblical understanding that my then catholic

Sunday school teacher did not understand. I say this because I asked questions that she was unable to answer. I was 16 years of age before I realized it was God talking to me through the words of Jeremiah. I came to understand later in life, it was a divine encounter.

One day as I walked to choir rehearsal, I experienced what was my first spiritual encounter. Literally, I could see a devil-like figure on my left shoulder and an angel-like figure on my right shoulder. The devil figure said to me, "you don't have to go over to that church God is not real, go and hang out with your friends." As I looked towards my left to see who was talking to me, I felt an eerie presence. The angel-like figure did not say anything, but stayed there as if to protect me. I continued walking, suddenly turned to my left and said aloud "LEAVE ME ALONE!" Then I felt a peace come over me and I continued on to choir rehearsal. I thought little about it after that day. Now, I know I was living the scripture James 4:7 NKJV that says, *"Therefore submit to God. Resist the devil and he will flee from you."*

I had a strong desire to read, understand and teach the Word of God, mainly because I got so much from the Word. I did not fully understand at that time the depth of it all. At the age of 19, I started teaching a youth group at the church that I attended. During this time, the Lord used me to reach and teach in a profound way. The ages I taught were 13-18, just a little younger than I was. I could see the transformation of the lives of these young people and the Lord gave me great revelation to share with the group that made an awesome impact on their personal relationships with the Lord.

A few years later, I encountered a divine experience during an alter call at Church. I had left the church and gone back into the world. After a few years, the Lord brought me back to the church. One day I was at the altar praying and asking God for more of Him. I remember the tears streaming down my face and the next thing I knew I was on the floor, hands extended up to the Lord. The most significant thing that stood out was a light that seemingly shone from the heavens directly to my forehead. I saw myself in a flowing white wedding gown. I heard the voice of the Lord saying to me, "you are my Bride of Christ". I was one of many in the church identified as the Bride. We know that the Church is the ultimate Bride of Christ but we also have to understand each of us is the Church.

From that point on, I chased hard after the Lord, not as a perfect person, but as a person seeking perfection. It was during a powerful worship service when the Lord fully revealed Jeremiah 1:5

> *Chase the Lord not as perfect person, but a person seeking perfection.*

scripture to me. I was one of the ordained Ministers' (Teacher) in the Body of Christ set in place in this church. During this service, the music was loud, the worship was strong and I sensed the presence of the Lord. The Lord spoke to me and said, "This day I call you forth as my prophet to deliver the words that I give unto you. You shall prophesy and not be afraid, I called you before you were formed in your mother's womb; I sanctified you and set you apart for such a time as this."

Initially, I just stood there crying because I knew this was a special calling and that His voice was going to be even louder, but I was wrong. His voice came as a still, small, voice but I was able to hear it clearly in the midst of a loud world. I will admit, there were times where I felt like Jonah and did not want to say what thus said the Lord. But, I was also like Jeremiah 20:9, where the word was like a burning fire in my heart and I could not help but speak it. I fully accepted the call of God for my life and I have not turned back from it to this day.

God Guides by His Word

Father God wants to see you succeed and move forward into the destiny He has prepared for you. It can be difficult at times to know how God is leading you. At the same time, following the Lord through His Word can be easy when you apply His Word accordingly. The Bible has much to say about directions for your life, In Proverbs 16:9 (ESV) it says, *"The heart of man plans his way, but the Lord established his steps."* What the Word says here is man meditates, prepares and plans their life; but God determines if or when the plan(s) are completed. God establishes our steps, and by "establish" it means; to bring into being or recognized.

Not everything that you plan will come to pass or happen the way you plan it. You may be thinking, why make plans? That is a good question. The short answer is, God gives everyone a free will. This "free will" allows you to decide to follow Him. God, will not force you to follow Him. However, when you do not then you need to be prepared for the consequences that life deals you without the Lord.

The Bible further says in Psalms 119:105 (ESV) *"Your word is a lamp to my feet and a light to my path."* Which simply means that the Word of God shows you the way to go, both day and night providing a lighted path. This scripture is also connected to Proverbs 6:23 (ESV) that says, *"For the commandment is a lamp, and the teaching a light, and the reproofs of discipline are the way of life."* This is known as the commandment that harmonizes with the will of God for your life. The law is the entire law of God's system of general instructions, which stands for the relationship of "lamp and light".

Therefore, when you consider "commandment" and the "law" in conjunction it enlightens your conscience and enables you to walk in God's way of life. In Psalm 119:105 above and Psalms 19:8 (ESV) it clearly says, *"...the precepts of the Lord are right, rejoicing the heart; the commandment of the Lord is pure, enlightening the eyes..."* This means to direct and show the true way of the Lord. God wants you to be happy, therefore, rejoicing of the heart, meaning what God has for you, are not stern commandments but gracious invitations to follow Him as His laws enlighten you and give revelation to your intellect.

In Isiah 58:11 (NLT) the Bible says, *"The Lord will guide you continually, giving you water when you are dry and restoring your strength. You will be like a well-watered garden, like an ever-flowing spring."* Again, here is a confirmation that God will direct your path and teach you the way to go in your down seasons, your times of depression and weariness. He will sustain you and strengthen you and you will be like a well-watered garden that produces good fruit. There is no water like the spiritual water supply from the Lord. It will never run dry.

The Bible further teaches:

John 14:26 (NIV)	John 16:13 (NIV)
But the Advocate, the Holy Spirit, whom the Father will send in my name, will teach you all things and will remind you of everything I have said to you.	*But when he, the Spirit of truth, comes, he will guide you into all the truth. He will not speak on his own; he will speak only what he hears, and he will tell you what is yet to come.*

As you can see here, the Word continues to confirm that the Lord will teach and guide you as well as remind you of His word. As you go through life dealing with different situations, the Holy Spirit will guide you to the truth. For example, when someone is attempting to cheat you or take advantage of you, the Holy Spirit will speak to you what He hears from God in order for you to make a sound decision concerning the situation.

Sometimes you will get a "check" in your spirit or your heart signifying that something about this person or deal is just not right. Then you have to make a decision if you want to proceed or back off.

How will this happen? God has many ways of giving you direction in life. Some are similar to the previous chapters; others can be in dreams as you sleep. He can guide you with open visions whereas you see it play out in what may seem like a daydream. God can use strangers in conversations to speak into your life and you walk away feeling like you have been in that scenario before. God can use His Prophets to prophesy to you and of course the preached Word as if it was designed just for you.

> God can use strangers in conversations to speak into your life

Do not limit "how" you will receive direction from God just be open to hear from Him in various ways. You want to be as the Word says in Proverbs 11:14 (NIV) it says, *"For lack of guidance a nation falls, but victory is won through many advisers."* As well as Proverbs, 1:5 (NIV) *"Let the wise listen and add to their learning, and let the discerning get guidance."* These scriptures speaks for themselves and indicates that you want to get Godly guidance, counsel and advice as you make decisions for your life.

Therefore, when you are going through any of life's previously listed issues whether it is divorce, loss of a loved one or persecution, it will be wise to seek the appropriate godly professional counselling to confide in as well as continual prayer for yourself. In doing so, you will receive the necessary guidance to help you move pass your past. Wise counsel can help you heal and help you deal with on-going or recurring issues. Keep in mind, not everyone you meet will be the "wise counselor" to offer you sound advice.

One important spiritual trait that will help you is to develop discernment. What is discernment? Discernment is to perceive by sight or, some other sense of judgement or perception. It is the quality of being able to grasp and comprehend what is obscure. When you have spiritual discernment, you will have the ability to see what is not evident to the average mind. You will be able to perceive the character and motives of others.

Another way discernment will help you is hearing the voice of God. That is being able to discern God's voice from the noises of the world and the devils voice. The ability to discern is a spiritual gift as defined in the Bible in 1 Corinthians 12:4-11 (NKJV), *"[4] There are diversities of gifts, but the same Spirit. [5] There are differences of ministries, but the same Lord. [6] And there are diversities of activities, but it is the same God who works all in all. [7] But the manifestation of the Spirit is given to each one for the profit of all: [8] for to one is given the word of wisdom through the Spirit, to another the word of knowledge through the same Spirit, [9] to another faith by the same Spirit, to another gifts of healings by the same Spirit, [10] to another the* *working of miracles, to another prophecy, to another discerning of spirits, to another different kinds of tongues, to another the interpretation of tongues. ^{11} But one and the same Spirit works all these things, distributing to each one individually as He wills."*

With that being said, you should always desire the spiritual gifts that God has provided to the Body of Christ that will assist you in living for Him in this life.

Chapter 4: How do I Follow the Voice of God?

When you have decisions to make about your life, it can sometimes feel quite difficult or confusing. You are not sure which way to go or to whom you should talk or listen. There are many people talking and many things said that are spoken with the intent to be advisable, but may be misleading and hurtful. Therefore, you want to seek the leading of the Lord for direction. You begin by praying to the Lord and asking Him to show you the way. Prayer is as a bi-directional communication between you and God. You pray, God listens and responds; then God speaks, and you listen and respond.

However, most people struggle to know if what they are hearing is really God's voice. Generally, if you are unsure you are hearing God voice then, you will not understand what He is saying to you. When you do not understand Him, then are you unable to follow Him. When you are unable to follow the Lord then you cannot reach your destiny. So, let us dig a little deeper into how to actually hear and follow God's voice.

You Must Recognize God's Voice

Let us consider this example. When a baby is born, their development is immature. They have to learn their parent's voice, and then distinguish mom from dad, and then parents from other voices. Sometimes this can be a challenge for a baby especially when auntie's voice sounds so much like mommy's voice. However, at some point, the baby will begin to recognize the difference. The baby will spend more time with mommy than auntie; mommy cares for the baby, feed the baby and talk to the baby more consistently. The more the baby hears mommy voice the more the baby begins to recognize mommy's voice from aunties' voice.

A mother's interaction with her baby brings about a very strong connection and a nurturing experience that fosters protection, encouragement and trust; especially during the time, the baby is in its developmental and training stages. As time goes on the baby develops into a child and when hearing mommy's voice can detect certain tones, like happiness, sadness, teaching and discipline. The child also begins to learn to respond to mommy in particular ways. Sometimes a child readily does what mommy asks. At times, the child will ignore what mommy says as if they did not hear. Other times, the child will rebel against what mom says although they fully understand what mommy asked of them. We see here as a child they are fully capable of recognizing mommy's voice and then take actions accordingly. You too must go through a process with similar methodologies to get to a place where you recognize God's voice.

How will that happen? You will hear God's voice more clearly, as you spend time with Him. This is accomplished by reading, meditating and searching the Word of God. The more you know His Word, the better you will recognize His voice. As you spend time in the Word your spirit will begin to develop an "ear to hear", what the Spirit of God is saying. You will start to distinguish His voice from the world, the enemy and other voices.

An example of hearing God through His word

When you are feeling down right angry about being divorced, you may even be bitter towards your ex-spouse. Because you just knew, he/she was the right one, but he/she cheated on you! Then during a time of flipping through the Bible, the Lord speaks to you, He tells you to forgive your ex and gives you Ephesians 4:31-32 (NKJV) that says, *"Let all bitterness, wrath, anger, clamor, and evil speaking be put away from you, with all malice. ³²And be kind to one another, tenderhearted, forgiving one another, even as God in Christ forgave you."*

As the baby in the earlier example, you have to decide "how" you will respond. Will you readily obey? Will you act as if you did not hear Him? What about if the Lord spoke to you from this scripture, how would you respond? Matthew 18:21-22 (KNJV) *"Then Peter came to Him and said, "Lord, how often shall my brother sin against me, and I forgive him? Up to seven times?" ²²Jesus said to him, "I do not say to you, up to seven times, but up to seventy times seven."*

The Word of God is very clear in its directions, when you allow the Lord to speak to you through it. The Bible says this in

Colossians 3:16, (NKJV) *"Let the word of Christ dwell in you richly in all wisdom, teaching and admonishing one another in psalms and hymns and spiritual songs, singing with grace in your hearts to the Lord."*

In this scripture, you literally "allow" the Word of God to develop your character, and wisdom as He teaches you through His word. We are teachers one to another as we share what the Lord gives each of us. As the Word dwells in you, it will counsel you in your decisions. He, God, brings His word back to you as a reminder of His promises to you.

Furthermore, when you consider knowing, hearing and following the voice of God, take into account John 10:27 KJV that says, *"My sheep hear my voice, and I know them, and they follow me."* What is in this scripture?

a. My Sheep – represents followers of Christ
b. Hear my voice – indicates followers recognizes the voice of God
c. I Know them – indicative of the Lord's response to followers of the faith who received Him
d. They follow me – implies or says as a follower of Christ, you are led by the Word, you recognize and follow the Word

So what is the overall analogy? Like a baby who has to learn their mother's voice, you as a believer must learn to hear

the voice of God. You must understand what His voice is saying to you in order to obey His voice. In hearing God's voice, you will be able to discern in your spirit when He says,
- "Stop, do not go any further"
- "Wait, take caution I am preparing a way"
- "Go, proceed the way has been made clear for you"

These signs will be clearer to you as you continue growing in your personal relationship with the Lord.

Sometimes you have to meditate on the Word, in doing so your spiritual mind will develop an internal voice that you will recognize as God's voice. What you hear or how you hear it will not necessarily be the same as what or how another person hears God. To meditate on scripture is to ponder and think about it until it is clear what the Lord is saying. Scripture is the written voice of God and is the primary way He speaks to you. Meditation on the scripture will lead you to prayer. Psalm 119:15-16 (NKJV) says, *"I will meditate on Your precepts, And contemplate Your ways. ¹⁶ I will delight myself in Your statutes; I will not forget Your word."* Again, meditating on the Word of God will activate it in your life and manifest itself in the way you respond to situations, why? Because you heard it and obeyed it.

> *Scripture is the written voice of GOD.*

You must understand God Voice

Like most people, you can read the Bible repeatedly and yet still do not fully understand how to apply what you have read to your life. Psalm 119:27 (NKJV) says, *"Make me understand the way of Your precepts; So shall I meditate on Your wonderful works."* Here, the writer is longing to have perfect knowledge of the Word of God or God's Law. Therefore, you should not only want to hear God's voice but you should also desire to understand what He is saying. Otherwise, there is no benefit to you and you will not be inclined to do as the scripture says, *"talk of His wondrous works"*. When you obtain an understanding of the Word of God, it activates you. It moves you into action.

Practical Steps in Hearing God's Voice

The Bible says in Matthew 7:7-8 (NKJV), *"Ask, and it will be given to you; seek, and you will find; knock, and it will be opened to you. ⁸ For everyone who asks receives, and he who seeks finds, and to him who knocks it will be opened."*

➢ Ask of God in communion:
- Pray with expectation from God, make your request known to Him.
- Have a conversation with God just as you would with your friend or spouse.

- This is your quiet time with Him; tell him what is on your heart and on your mind.
- Tell Him about your day, how good or bad your day has been.
- Be available to hear what He has to say.
- Ask Him to explain His word to you.
- Ask Him to show you the way in your marriage, your career etc. Ask Him anything you want to ask.
- His promise is if you ask, you will receive.

➤ Seek God:
- Seeking God means, if you are expecting something, you will find something.
- Do not pray and jump up. Rest in His presence and allow Him to speak to you.
- As He speaks scriptures to you, look them up while in His presence, meditate on them and allow Him to give you revelation concerning them.
- The answer from scripture will provide the guidance that you are seeking.
- Look for God to show up in ways that are different, unimaginable, and peculiar.
- Do not stop seeking God for the answers to your situation, be patient.

➤ Knock on Doors:
- Knocking on doors, first the door to God means you are expecting Him to open the doors of Heaven.
- Knocking is another form of prayer with fervency and persistency.

- Knock until the door opens and the Lord lets you in on the solution, the blessing and the provision.
- Knock until Father God releases from Heaven the very thing you desire.
- When He shows you the directions, the way to go, be obedient and follow. He knows what is best for you.

These are some practical steps and there are other ways to learn to hear and follow the voice of God. As He birth in you other avenues, pursue them vigorously. Remember, Psalm 3:5-6 (NKJV) says, *"Trust in the Lord with all your heart, And lean not on your own understanding; ⁶ In all your ways acknowledge Him, And He shall direct your paths."*

Chapter 5: Arriving in Destiny!

Did you know your destiny is awaiting your arrival? Are you still willing to get there? God has a destiny for you and He wants you to walk into it. Your destiny was created especially for you and is different from the next person's destiny; even if it appears to look the same. Destiny is the events that will necessarily happen to a particular person or thing in the future. It is the hidden power believed to control what will happen in the future. Fate is a predetermined, usually inevitable course of events.

Everyone has a destiny. The key is, you have to believe there is a destiny and understand it is a journey to get there. How you get there will definitely differ from how someone else will get there. Your journey can take you down many paths before you arrive. Therefore, you want to be as prepared as possible. Some preparation entails healing from past hurts, pains, and issues that have held you captive and prevented you from moving forward. Like bad relationships, divorce, loss of loved ones and personal persecution.

On the Road to Destiny!

Imagine your life being like a road trip. You know your GPS tells you your route will take eight hours. It maps out the course of the roads and provides the direction you should take. You have packed your bags, your goodies and your favorite road music. As you hit the road, you have high hopes that your travels will go according to plan. You have calculated the rest stops, which include gas stations. You have crossed every "T" and dotted every "I". You feel confident this journey will go without a hitch.

Suddenly, you hear a loud noise and your vehicle starts to rock. You pull over to examine the issue. You discover a nail in your tire! You think, okay no worries there is a spare tire in the trunk. You will simply change the tire and be on your way. It takes about a half hour; but you think you can make the time up on the open road.

Well, what do you know; the spare tire was swapped out for a donut tire! You are thinking there is no way I will be able to get very far on a donut tire. This will surely push you back on your arrival to your destination. Unfortunately, you have to use the donut tire to get off the road to a tire shop before they close. This is just another setback because the doors to the nearest tire shop just closed for the night.

So, at this point, you must decide, will you give up and turn around or will you pursue other options to get around the tire obstacle? In life, you will face obstacles. They come in the form of bad relationships, marital issues, divorce, loss of loved ones and even persecution. Just like the road trip and the blown tire, it slows you down for a season but rarely will it stop you. For obstacles to stop you, it requires you to give up and no longer look for options and accept the bad fate.

The Bible says that your faith is going to be tested through the trials that you go through. James 1:2-4 (TPT) says, *"My fellow believers, when it seems as though you are facing nothing but difficulties, see it as an invaluable opportunity to experience the greatest joy that you can!* ^{3} *For you know that when your faith is tested it stirs up power within you to endure all things.* ^{4} *And then as your endurance grows even stronger it will release perfection into every part of your being until there is nothing missing and nothing lacking."* These verses start out letting you know that you "will" face difficulties and troubles, but how will you respond? How will you handle difficulties, adversities and calamity when it is starring you in the face?

Peter says, in verse two to "consider it an opportunity for great joy…" What? You may be thinking I should be happy in the midst of trouble! Yes, you should be happy, because the issue is an opportunity for the Lord to work in your life. You should expect to be over joyed with the outcome because the scripture further tells you the testing of your faith will grow your ability to endure. Where endurance grows, it enables you to become capable of handling the trials of life without it taking you out; knocking you down or stopping your forward momentum. This joy however, as spoken above relates to the experience you encounter when the Lord takes care of your situation.

Your tire blew out, the nearest tire shop just closed. You are faced with a dreaded decision. However, to experience the joy in this situation is when a total stranger, who happened to have the same make and model of your vehicle; approach you and offers assistance. The stranger did not just change your tire, but gave you a perfectly usable spare tire! The stranger had purchased two new tires the day before and did not need the extra tire. This situation is a description of a divine encounter. God can intervene on your behalf!

The Bible teaches in Hebrews 13:2 (NLT), *"Don't forget to show hospitality to strangers, for some who have done this have entertained angels without realizing it!"* God sends angels to assist you along the way to your destiny. Some people may feel it is happenstance. However, special encounters have a way of allowing you to see it as a divine intervention that only God could orchestrate.

You are back on track heading to your destiny. Feeling relieved the past ordeal is behind you. Or, so you thought. As you seemingly gain traction on moving forward, yet another obstacle gets in the way that affects your progress. On your roadway is a fatal crash. Traffic moving in your direction has slowed down to a crawl and movement is extremely slow. You know you must keep going but the lane you are in has no exit for miles.

It just so happens that you find yourself on Greif Lane. Mourning the death of a marriage or the death of a loved one. You want to keep moving but you find life has become a stop and go ordeal. Sometimes, you are moving at a good pace, other times you are at a very slow pace and other times you find yourself at a complete stand still. No movement, nothing happening. You cannot see the road ahead, all you see are red lights.

While these obstacles are in your path, God is still making a way for you to continue to move forward to your destiny. Even when you cannot see the way, the way is there. The promises of God are still available to you. Psalms 23:4 (TPT) says, *"Lord, even when your path takes me through the valley of deepest darkness, fear will never conquer me, for you already have! You remain close to me and lead me through it all the way. Your authority is my strength and my peace. The comfort of your love takes away my fear. I'll never be lonely, for you are near."*

As you can see from this verse, you are never alone. Even when you think, you are in the darkest place of your life; the promise of God is that He has conquered your fears with His love. His authority leads the way to your strength and your peace. He further promises that you will never be alone because He is always near you. There is great comfort knowing, even when you are by yourself, you are not alone.

As you get back on the road to destiny, keep in mind as the Lord heals you from past pains, it does not mean you are beyond the point of ever experiencing pain or disappointments. What it does mean, is you have learned how to deal with those situations differently.

You Have Arrived at Destiny!

You see the evidence that you are arriving at your destination. The signs are clear, the road is clear of obstacles. The anticipation of arrival is insurmountable! The joy of finally being free from the past makes way for great hope and opportunity.

You are here, in your destiny. Now what? What are you going to do? How do you do what you believe you are destined to do? You know what God has placed in your hands. It is all in your head and your heart. So, why do you feel insecure about doing it? Why is the feeling of inadequacy looming over you?

The simple answer that Jesus gave is in John 10:10 (TPT) that says, *"A thief has only one thing in mind—he wants to steal, slaughter, and destroy. But I have come to give you everything in abundance, more than you expect—life in its fullness until you overflow!"* Understand this, just because you made it to the place of destiny, does not mean the devil is going to stop and let you be successful. He, the devil, will fight you all the way. He will try to bring you back to the place of brokenness, heartaches, the "why" of your divorce, death of a loved one or even try to persecute you to the point whereas you doubt the plan of God for your life.

Jesus reminds you of the intentions of the devil. Why? So that you can be aware of his tactics to steal your peace of mind, steal your joy and steal your assignment. Jesus further reminds you that the intent of the devil is to utterly slaughter or kill you. First, through your faith, by planting doubt and unbelief; then, through killing your will to go on or dream big.

If you allow the devil to discourage you, then he has succeeded in destroying you. However, the Word of God tells you that the devil has already been defeated. You are blessed and the devil cannot curse who or what the Lord has blessed.

> *The devil has already been defeated*

In your season of God ordained destiny, you may not know exactly what to expect or how it should look. However, there are some common things you can do to ensure you stay on the road to your destiny. Just to name a few, you should:

- Know who you are
- Know why you were born
- Understand your purpose
- Have discovered your talent / strength / gifts
- Have tapped into what you are truly passionate about

You know you have arrived at your destiny when the "thing" that truly gives you meaning of your life, is what you are doing. Every issue, pain, and problem you have ever experienced pointed you to where you are in your destiny. Every road travelled has led you to this place. You realize the energy you get when you are performing the "thing" that you are meant to do. You are happy doing it and nothing can be more joyful than doing it.

While you are experiencing the best time of your life, it will not be without struggles and challenges. Do not think it will be an easy ride to success. The devil is still lurking, roaming and seeking whom he can devour, it may well be you! When you do find the devil throwing things your way, remember to apply the following in order to keep moving forward when the pressure is on:

- Prayer
- Wise Counsel
- Strategic Planning
- Perseverance to push forward

You are in your destiny! Now stay on track as we dive deeper into things you can do to stay on track.

Chapter 6: How to Stay on Destiny's Track

Have you ever felt like you were just where the Lord would have you and then your world is turned upside down? You wonder how can these things be happening when you have been obedient to the Lord doing everything He told you to do. Yet, things are still going awry.

Well as mentioned in previous chapters, the enemy, the "devil", comes to kill, steal and destroy. However, you must learn to rely on the second half of what Jesus says in John 10:10b (TPT) that says, *"...But I have come to give you everything in abundance, more than you expect—life in its fullness until you overflow!* Keep this scripture in mind whenever the enemy tries to discourage you in your assignment, his purpose is to distract you. However, Jesus came to provide for you everything you need, moreover, in **abundance**! That is more than you expect. Your life, as you are led by the Holy Spirit, will be full and overflowing and that is something to be excited about!

As you continue in your walk in and through your destiny, let us look at some key points that will help keep you moving forward. This is by no means a complete exhaustive list. However, it will be enough to get you going as the Lord reveals more of His plan for you.

- Prayer
- Wise Counsel

- Strategic Planning
- Perseverance to push forward

How does Prayer keep you on track?

Have you ever heard the term "The mind is a battlefield"? There is truth in this statement, because, if the enemy can keep your mind off the things the Lord has for you, then you will get off track. How does this happen? The consistent bombarding of your mind with your past. The enemy wants you to dwell on your failed relationship, divorce or persecutions. He wants you to feel sorry for yourself; he wants you to feel like a total failure.

Therefore, he keeps rehashing in your mind "how" it all went down. He slurs accusations of how it was your fault. Why? Because the enemy is "the accuser". He wants your mind preoccupied with stuff that prevents you from focusing on what is ahead for you. You cannot move forward looking backward.

> *You cannot move forward looking backward*

Therefore, you have to pray the Word of God over your mind. Romans 12:1-2 (TPT) says, *"Beloved friends, what should be our <u>proper response to God's</u> marvelous mercies? I encourage you to <u>surrender yourselves to God</u> to be his sacred, living sacrifices. And live in holiness, experiencing all that delights his heart. For this becomes your genuine expression of worship.*

*²Stop imitating the ideals and opinions of the culture around you, but <u>be inwardly **transformed** by the Holy Spirit through a total reformation of how you **think**</u>. This will <u>empower you to discern God's will</u> as you live a beautiful life, satisfying and perfect in his eyes."* You can discover a few things from this:

- The proper response to God is to surrender yourself to Him
- Be transformed by the renewing of your mind by how you think
- Be empowered to discern God's will, in doing so, the enemy will not be able to over-power your thought life

Furthermore, when you actually pray this scripture the transformation process begins. Your focus will begin to change. As your thoughts come into alignment with the Word of God, the enemy will have less power and ammunition to alter your thoughts. Then you will have the power to stand firm and say to the devil, "it is under the blood" and he cannot accuse you of the things the Lord have forgiven.

The enemy will bring up your past all the time. However, you must fight using the Word of God. If he is trying to make you go back into depression, quote and pray these scriptures and similar ones:

1. Philippians 4:6-7

2. Psalm 46:1; 10

1. Philippians 4:6-7 (NIV) says, *"Do not be anxious about anything, but in every situation, by prayer and petition, with thanksgiving, present your requests to God. ⁷And the peace of God, which transcends all understanding, will guard your hearts and your minds in Christ Jesus."*

In essence, this scripture tells you not to allow worry and fear to pull you in all kinds of direction, causing you to be confused and dishearten about your directions. Instead, you should saturate yourself with prayer throughout the day, building up your faith. Do not be afraid to be honest with the Lord and tell Him how you really feel. As you pray this scripture, you will learn to be at peace in where you are and what you are destined to do. You must guard your mind and heart from the attacks of the enemy.

Do your best not to allow anxiety to flood your mind. Your process in destiny takes time. You should not allow the feeling of being behind or inadequate control your state of mind or alter your destiny. Remember, the Word of God says, when anxiety is trying to overtake you then you take it to the Lord in prayer with a thankful heart. You will find that this is an opportunity to see the hand of God move mightily in your situation.

When you truly give the issues and mind attacks to the Lord your will experiences His peace. People would wonder how you are at peace with the various things going on in your life. It is a "But GOD" kind of life. He declared in His word, it is the "Peace of God" guarding your heart and mind as you stay in Christ Jesus!

2. Psalm 46:1; 10a says, *"¹ God is our refuge and strength, an ever-present help in trouble ¹⁰ᵃ He says, "Be still, and know that I am God..."*

In a refuge, the Lord God provides and acts as a place of shelter, security and safety. You can turn to Him when trouble is all around you, especially when the enemy is attacking your thoughts; you have to bring those thoughts under control by keeping and focusing your mind on the Lord through His word. Let this mind be in you, which is also in Christ Jesus (Philippians 2:5). Be motivated by the example that Christ Jesus set, that is to truly humble your thoughts to Him taking on His type of mindset.

Let's look at what Paul says in 2 Corinthians 10:3-5 (TPT), *"³⁻⁴For although we live in the natural realm, we don't wage a military campaign employing human weapons, using manipulation to achieve our aims. Instead, our spiritual weapons are energized with divine power to effectively dismantle the defenses behind which people hide. ⁵ We can demolish every deceptive fantasy that opposes God and break through every arrogant attitude that is raised up in defiance of the true knowledge of God. We capture, like prisoners of war, every thought and insist that it bow in obedience to the Anointed One."*

What you are experiencing is spiritual warfare in the supernatural, but it affects you in the natural realm. You must understand you cannot fight a spiritual battle with natural weapons. Even if the enemy is using your ex-spouse, co-workers or parishioners. The scripture above indicates their attitudes are in defiance of the true knowledge of GOD. Therefore, you use spiritual weapons to do battle in this war, which is a deceptive fantasy attempting to stop you from moving forward in your destiny.

> *Deceptive fantasies are an attempt to stop you from moving forward*

The main war you face is the battle of your mind. So, Paul explains in verse five, when the enemy is waging war on you with thoughts from your past, it is intended to defy the Word of God and try to make you believe a lie from your past. However, the Word of God, your spiritual weapon, tells you to be like a prisoner of war. Capture the negative thoughts the enemy sends and bring them under subjection or bow them down under the obedience of Jesus Christ. You must trust and believe what the Word of God says to you over the thoughts the enemy sends.

How does Wise Counsel keep you on track?

When considering wisdom, you cannot help but to think of the state of being wise. First and foremost, understand that wisdom comes from God. James 1:5 (TPT) says, *"And if anyone longs to be wise, ask God for wisdom and he will give it! He won't see your lack of wisdom as an opportunity to scold you over your failures but he will overwhelm your failures with his generous grace."* You cannot be afraid to ask the Lord for help on an assignment that He gives you. He will not see you as a failure or as someone who cannot get it right. He wants you to ask, He wants you to do your assignment. He has your back on it. In fact, He has graced you to do your assignment.

Depending on your assignment, the Lord will put a mentor in your pathway who can provide details and be a guide as you walk through your assignment. The purpose of the mentor is to share their knowledge with you. In doing so, you will become wiser concerning your assignment. Proverbs 19: 20 (AMP) says, *"Listen to counsel, receive instruction, and accept correction, that you may be wise in the time to come."*

Although there will be times where you feel you have things under control or all figured out, still humble yourself and receive the wise counsel. When you do, you will discover the advice is very useful just when you need it.

Heeding to godly wise counsel allows you to receive from the Lord what you may otherwise miss. Especially, when you are stressing, anxious and feeling overwhelmed about your assignment. Your godly counselor should be operating according to Isaiah 11:2 (NIV) that says, *"The Spirit of the Lord will rest on him—the Spirit of wisdom and of understanding, the Spirit of counsel and of might, the Spirit of the knowledge and fear of the Lord...*" Therefore, when the counselor is operating in the spirit of counsel, they should also have the spirit of wisdom and knowledge flowing. This will keep them grounded in the Word of God with honesty and integrity that you will benefit from.

How do Strategic Plans keep you on track?

Most people arrive in destiny just to find shortly afterwards, they lack direction and are set up to fail. This is where the term "when you fail to plan, you plan to fail" comes from. The Lord does not give you an assignment for your destiny without giving you a strategy. In Jeremiah 29:11 (NIV) it says, *"For I know the plans I have for you," declares the Lord, "plans to prosper you and not to harm you, plans to give you hope and a future."* Notice in this verse the Lord uses the word "plans" three times. Plans are a method or schema on doing, acting or proceeding to something. With the three plans used here, the Lord wants you to know that:

    I.   He knows your plans
    II. He plans to prosper you
    III. His plans provide you with hope (desire to be fulfilled)
    IV. His plans bring you into the future (destiny)

Therefore, if God knows your plans then He has a strategy to get it accomplished.

Consider "strategy", it is a plan, a method or series of moves or stratagems to reach a specific goal or result. Even when you cannot see the plans or the hand of God moving, He has already moved in your favor. His plan was set in motion long before you knew or understood you ever had a destiny.

> *Even when you cannot see God moving, He has already moved in your favor*

Just because the Lord knows your plan does not mean you are excluded from doing anything outside of arriving in your destiny. Habakkuk 2:2 (NKJV) says this, *"Then the Lord answered me and said: "Write the vision And make it plain on tablets, That he may run who reads it."* Writing down the vision (strategy) is your portion of the overall strategic plan for your destiny and assignment. As the Lord speaks to you concerning your assignment, you should write it down in a logical, executable, and sequential order that is readable and understandable.

There will be times you will have a thought; you will think it is your own; however, it is really the Lord speaking to you. Do not discharge it as nothing. Remember, the vision is yet for an appointed time. As you are writing your plan, do not doubt your plan or strategy.

How does Perseverance keep you on track?

Consider "MOVE", it is to pass from one place or position to another. It is an action word; therefore, you must do something. You should be compelled by Isaiah 43:18-19 (NKJV) that says, *"Do not remember the former things, Nor consider the things of old. ^{19}Behold, I will do a new thing, now it shall spring forth; shall you not know it? I will even make a road in the wilderness and rivers in the desert."*

The former things that happened in your past, try to hold you back and not allow you to move forward. God wants you to forget them. Forget the pain associated with divorce or broken relationships. You do not forget your lost loved ones, but you do forget your dependency on them that has crippled you and held you back. Let the pain from the persecution go and forgive them.

Part of perseverance is being able to forgive as Jesus forgave those that persecuted Him in Luke 23:34 *"While they were nailing Jesus to the cross, he prayed over and over, "Father, forgive them, for they don't know what they're doing.""* Therefore, you must do what the Word says in Matthew 6:15, it speaks the same thing to you as a believer that says, *"And when you pray, make sure you forgive the faults of others so that your Father in heaven will also forgive you. ^{15}But if you withhold forgiveness from others, your Father withholds* *forgiveness from you."* You must forgive in order to receive the new thing the Lord wants to do and continue in your life.

When you begin to persevere towards staying on track, you will see and experience another level of persistence. You grab a solid hold to what God has called you to do and you give it all you have. Hebrews 10:36 (NIV) says, *"You need to persevere so that when you have done the will of God, you will receive what he has promised."* Therefore, push forward without looking back so that you may receive the reward and promises of God.

So now, the question is...
- Do you want to remain your destiny?
- Are you ready to run your race?
- Are you going to leave the past behind?
- Are you ready to receive your victorious prize through Christ Jesus?

Then keep your eyes on YOUR prize and don't compare yourself to another person even if their assignment is very similar.

The Word of the Lord says to you in Psalm 37:1-5 (NLT) *"Don't worry about the wicked or envy those who do wrong. ²For like grass, they soon fade away. Like spring flowers, they soon wither. ³Trust in the Lord and do good. Then you will live safely in the land and prosper. ⁴Take delight in the Lord, and he will give you your heart's desires. ⁵Commit everything you do to the Lord. Trust him, and he will help you."* Bottom line, put your trust in the Lord and you will live a safe and prosperous life. Delight in the Lord and you will receive the desires of your heart. Lastly, when you commit everything to the Lord and truly trust Him, He will help you to stay on assignment and on point in your destiny.

Chapter 7: Healing in the Emotions

When we think of healing, generally it is with the understanding that it is a physical healing. That is from a sickness or disease like cold, flu, cancer, diabetes, internal organs etc. However, have you considered healing in your emotions?

Emotions are an instructive state of mind deriving from one's circumstance, mood or relationship with others. Emotions are synonymous with your feelings. Your emotions deal with physiological experiences that affect the mind and cause an adverse phenomena reaction to the situation. Sometimes the phenomenal event(s) can or will cause your emotions to react in such a way that one can become emotionally ill. Such as becoming irrational, having uncontrollable fears, persistent anxiety or extreme hostility. Some signs of emotional illness can be:

- Extreme personality changes
- Agitation
- Withdrawal
- Decline in personal care of oneself
- Feeling of hopelessness

What I have seen and experienced from individuals' emotional state of mind is that sometimes they get fuzzy and confused about the circumstances they are facing. In turn, their thoughts concerning the issues become overwhelming and incomprehensible. When that happens one can experience emotional outbursts such as uncontrollable crying, intense anger, debilitating fear and more. Therefore, trying to control the emotion becomes a challenge. The more emotional one becomes, the more they are challenged.

Your Emotions can be healed!

How can healing take place in your emotions? When you are looking at a person from the outside, their appearance does not necessarily show their emotional state of mind. Why, because it is not a physical illness, it is internal, in the mind, in the heart and it must be dealt with differently. The first thing is for one to come to grips with the situation that has seemingly caused the onset of the emotional imbalance.

Let us discuss coming to grips with a circumstance. What does that look like? What will that entail? What will one have to do to come to grips? Everyone have different circumstances, but the rationale behind "coming to grips" can be very similar.

- Talk to a professional in the area(s) you are dealing with
- Do your best to understand what is going on in your personal circumstance(s)
- Do not play the blame game or accuse back and forth
- Calm down, destress and pull logical thinking back into play

Put yourself in the place of the other person or put yourself in the situation in which Paul the Apostle said after you have done all to stand; still stand! Ephesians 6:10-13 (KJV) says, *"Finally, my brethren, be strong in the Lord, and in the power of his might. Put on the whole armour of God, that ye may be able to stand against the wiles of the devil. For we wrestle not against flesh and blood, but against principalities, against powers, against the rulers of the darkness of this world, against spiritual wickedness in high places. Wherefore take unto you the whole armour of God, that ye may be able to withstand in the evil day, and having done all, to stand."* When you understand these verses, you will understand that it is principalities, powers, rulers of darkness of this world and spiritual wickedness in high places, that you are wrestling with in all your circumstance(s).

However, there is more to be understood about the spiritual side of emotional healing. 1 Peter 5:10 (ESV) says, *"And after you have suffered a little while, the God of all grace, who has called you to his eternal glory in Christ, will himself restore, confirm, strengthen, and establish you."* You see, He (God) did not leave you, during the time of suffering, you were trying to deal with the circumstance without Him (God); and that is what caused the suffering. His grace is sufficient!

When you remember you were called **out** of darkness to His eternal Glory, then you will be restored (back to where you are supposed to be in the Kingdom of God). You will be confirmed (validated by the Heavenly Father); strengthened (able to handle and stand in the adversity of circumstances); and established (shown to be valid and stable).

Psalm 34:19 says, (KJV) *"Many are the afflictions of the righteous: but the Lord delivereth him out of them all."* The afflictions, pain, suffering and mental distress brought on by emotional suffering, you, the righteous, will be delivered from them all by the power of the LORD! Again, you are not alone the Lord is with you!

God's plan of Healing for you

Remember Job of the Bible? He had more afflictions on him than one can ever imagine. However, here we see how God healed him and restored everything. Job 42:10-17 (NKJV) says, *"¹⁰ the Lord restored Job's losses when he prayed for his friends. Indeed the Lord gave twice as much as he had before. ¹¹Then all his brothers, all his sisters, and all those who had been his acquaintances before, came to him and ate food with him in his house; and they consoled him and comforted him for all the adversity that the Lord had brought upon him. Each one gave him a piece of silver and each a ring of gold. ¹²Now <u>the Lord blessed the latter days of Job more than his beginning</u>; for he had fourteen thousand sheep, six thousand camels, one thousand yoke of oxen, and one thousand female donkeys. ¹³He also had seven sons and three daughters. ¹⁴And he called the name of the first Jemimah, the name of the second Keziah, and* *the name of the third Keren-Happuch. ^{15}In all the land were found no women so beautiful as the daughters of Job; and their father gave them an inheritance among their brothers. ^{16}After this Job lived one hundred and forty years, and saw his children and grandchildren for four generations. ^{17}So Job died, old and full of days."* So during your time of emotional distress, know that when the Lord heals you He will restore to you, whatever you have lost, if you continue to bless Him and not curse Him.

Jeremiah 29:11 (ESV) says, *"For I know the plans I have for you, declares the Lord, plans for welfare and not for evil, to give you a future and a hope."* God has a plan for you and it has nothing to do with the overwhelming pain of emotional distress and broken-heartedness. He said His plan is for your good and not for evil, nor would it bring evil to you. His plan and purpose for you is to give you something to hope for, to believe in. Therefore, as you seek the Lord and give yourself to Him, He will show you His plans for you and order your steps toward them to bring you to a place of peace of mind.

3 John 1:2 (NKJV) declares, *"Beloved, I pray that you may prosper in all things and be in health, just as your soul prospers."* You see, the Lord wants you healed in every aspect of your life, body and soul. That is inclusive of your emotions; prosperity of your soul is to prosper in your emotions and your mind. God does not want you to be tormented in your emotions! This prayer has already gone out for you now all you have to do

> **The Lord wants you healed**

is receive it. How? You are righteous and Psalm 34:17 says. *"The righteous cry out, and the Lord hears, And delivers them out of all their troubles."* Therefore, believe and receive your healing in your emotions for a joyful heart is good medicine. God is your refuge and strength!

What will it take? FAITH!

When you are expecting God to heal you, it will require you to have, and exercise your faith. Faith described in Mark 11:22-24 (NKJV) says, *"So Jesus answered and said to them, "Have faith in God. For assuredly, I say to you, whoever says to this mountain, 'Be removed and be cast into the sea,' and does not doubt in his heart, but believes that those things he says will be done, he will have whatever he says. Therefore, I say to you, whatever things you ask when you pray, believe that you receive them, and you will have them."*

As you see, you have to do something to exercise your faith. The scripture says, **YOU** speak to the mountain (i.e. mountain of pain, sickness, disappointment, discouragement, etc.), do not doubt. But believe what you decree and declare and it will happen, then you will be in a position to receive your healing.

Matthew 15:28 (TPT) says, *"Then Jesus answered her, "Dear woman, your faith is strong! What you desire will be done for you." And at that very moment, her daughter was instantly set free from demonic torment."* You have to operate like this woman, even though Jesus was where he was for a different reason, she would not let that stop her from seeking healing for her tormented (emotion ill) daughter. She was driven and you should be also. You should do whatever it takes to get your healing in whatever area you desire.

Your ultimate faith resides in this scripture: Hebrews 11:1

NKJV	TPT	AMP
Now faith is the substance of things hoped for, the <u>evidence of things not seen</u>.	Now faith brings our hopes into reality and becomes <u>the foundation needed to acquire the things we long for</u>. It is all the evidence required to prove what is still unseen	Now faith is the assurance (title deed, confirmation) of things hoped for (divinely guaranteed), and the evidence of things not seen [the conviction of their reality—<u>faith comprehends as fact what cannot be experienced by the physical senses</u>].

Faith, it is known as, 'the NOW faith', and it delivers the things that you cannot see; it is the foundation needed to acquire the healing you long for. Faith comprehends and understand what you cannot physically experience with your natural senses. Your belief brings the manifestation of faith from heaven to earth for the thing(s) you are praying.

Lastly, do not waver in your faith, as it will delay the promises of God for your life. You have been justified by the

Lord and 2 Corinthians declares, *"For we walk by faith, not by sight."* It is not what you see but what you believe, because without Hebrews 11:6 (TPT) tells you, *"And without faith living within us it would be impossible to please God. <u>For we come to God in faith</u> knowing that he is real and that he rewards the faith of those who passionately seek him."*

Word from the Lord!

You Are Equipped

What is that you have in your hand? I summon you to look at what I have blessed you with. I have equipped you with the necessary tools to start, continue and complete the task in which I, the Lord, have given you to do.

Do not be afraid for today I give you the tenacity and boldness to step out; step out of your comfort zone. The boldness to approach; the boldness to speak; the boldness to do!

For the anointing is upon you to perform, do it now, do it swiftly, for I, the Lord, have opened doors no man can shut; closed doors no man can open.

The fear you walked under has been dispelled; I restore to you the ability to complete. I restore to you the excitement of your first task you received. I stir up the gifts within you; I pour this day into you all you need and I fill you up whereas you overflow.

I sent my Word to heal you, no longer shall you feel inadequate, insufficient, or beneath where I have called you to be. So, rise up, get up and move to the place I have destined for you.

Says the Lord,
Through His Servant
Prophet Frizella

The Just Shall

Sometimes we make decisions and choices in our life that not only affect us but it affects other people in our life, then think about it afterwards and condemn ourselves for saying, doing or deciding that thing. We misunderstand what the Bible says, "There is NOW no condemnation for those who belong to Christ Jesus." Romans 8:1 (KJV) When you belong to Christ you have been justified (free of quilt and pain associated with sin.)

Proverbs 24:16 teaches that a just man, woman, or person falls seven times and rise up again. When we repent and ask for forgiveness. We can stand on the Word of God that declares the just shall live by faith (Habakkuk 2:4; Hebrew 10:38, Romans 1:17).

Therefore, I encourage you to resist condemning yourself for past mistakes, decisions, or actions. You have been forgiven and justified by the Lord. You are His, therefore, you are not defined by your past. So, walk upright in the newness that has been provided to you.

Poem: He Can Be Found

I looked to God for strength
Thru the pain of each day
When I cannot find Him
I bow my knees to pray

I opened my eyes to see
The beauty he created in me
Just as I was ready to give up
Behold, the Lord showed up

Holy Spirit descended from above
To shower me with His Love
In my pain and to my surprise
I realized Jesus did arise

Don't look down
He won't be found
Because of His Love
He sits high above

When my dreams seem shattered
Jesus knew what mattered
When He spoke the special sound
Then I knew He can be found.

By Frizella Donegan Taylor

About the Author

𝕱𝖗𝖎𝖟𝖊𝖑𝖑𝖆 𝕯𝖔𝖓𝖊𝖌𝖆𝖓 𝕿𝖆𝖞𝖑𝖔𝖗 is a wife, mother, grandmother, Author, and Conference Speaker.

Frizella's writing career began over 20 years ago, and she has written and published three books to date. Which are; a new believer help book, a book of prayers and a 30-day devotional.

Frizella has also composed and written a prayer journal and several ministry tracks. Her Christian background has provided her with a wealth of leadership experiences (i.e. children's ministry, youth ministry, women ministry, prayer and intercessory ministry as well as Pastoral) to glean from and share.

Frizella's formal education includes a Master's degree in Information Technology, Bachelor of Science in Management and Business, and an Associate's degree in Computer Programming.

Frizella along with her husband, Steve are Co-Owners of TaylorMade Publishing LLC of Florida providing services to authors in the areas of coaching, proofreading, editing, formatting, eBook, flipbook and book publishing. You can learn more about TaylorMade Publishing LLC at www.TaylorMadePublishingFL.com.

About the Publisher

TaylorMade Publishing was created by Frizella and Steve Taylor, a husband and wife team. It was birthed from a desire to publish their books without surrendering their rights and royalties to the traditional publishing company. As authors who desired to publish and market their books, TaylorMade Publishing provides the resources to publish without the traditional hassles.

TaylorMade Publishing has developed a highly successful formula that allows new or established authors to choose services needed in order to get their books to market in the most efficient and economical way possible.

Our staff is committed to providing authors with an exceptional publishing experience, allowing them to focus their time and energy on their passion without the distractions, headaches and roadblocks often encountered in the publishing process.

Books by Frizella

Changes, Changes, Changes
God changes you into the image of Jesus by His Word

This book offers insight to a personal change in your Christian walk that helps your transformation to blossom into a beautiful butterfly. If you are ready to change your life, then this book will offer insights on how God wants to transform you into a new person to be used in His Kingdom.

Growing in the Lord sometimes bring challenges in our personal relationships. Here you will find some key points in dealing with these sensitive challenges. These key points will assist you with your personal growth in the Lord and help you discern relationships in your life.

- Understanding and receiving salvation
- Understanding and learning WHO Christ is
- Understanding and learning that your life can and will be transformed
- And much more

Author: Frizella Donegan
ISBN: 978-0-9968123-0-6

A Family That PRAYS
A Book of Prayers

The Bible teaches us that the effectual fervent prayer of the righteous avails much. However, what if one does not know how to pray or where to start? Where does that leave you? The disciples asked Jesus to teach them how to pray and today the Lord still teaches us how to pray and uses people to assist in that teaching.

In this book, you will find self-help prayers that will enable you to have a successful prayer life right away. You will learn how to pray effectively and get results. With a full understanding of what prayer is, it puts you on the right path of communicating with God. God is not moved by your tears, emotions or begging; God is moved by His Word...His Promises in His Word. Therefore, you are to pray His word back to Him.

Author: Frizella Donegan
ISBN: 978-0-9968123-2-0

Noon Break In to HIS Presence
30-Day Devotional

In Psalms 55, King David utters some profound words that deal with trusting in God. When you have to deal with treacherous people especially in the work place, sometimes you need a midday break through!

This devotional has 30 exhortations that help keep in you in perfect peace because your mind will stay on the Lord Jesus! Psalm 55:17 confirms that noonday devotion is well within order. It simply says "Evening, and morning, and at noon, will I pray, and cry aloud: and he shall hear my voice." For the next 30 days, you will have a quick word at your fingertips within this devotional. Then you can start over again as the Word take root in your heart and more revelation is given to you from the Lord.

Author: Frizella Taylor
ISBN: 978-0-9968123-3-7

www.ingramcontent.com/pod-product-compliance
Lightning Source LLC
Chambersburg PA
CBHW020736020526
44118CB00033B/954